Massachusetts Ecoregions

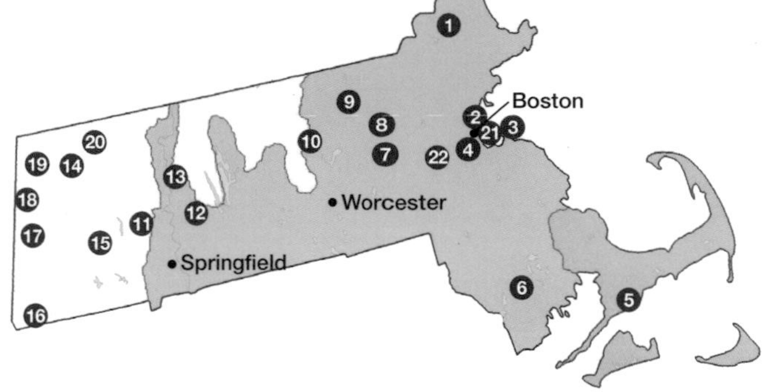
Northeastern Highlands
Northeastern Coastal Zone
Atlantic Coastal Pine Barrens
Boston
Worcester
Springfield
1
2
3
4
5
6
7
8
9
10
11
12
13
14
15
16
17
18
19
20
21
22

1. Maudslay State Park Newburyport
2. Boston Public Gardens
3. Boston Harbor Islands NRA
4. Blue Hills Reservation
5. Waquoit Bay National Estuarine Research Reserve
6. Freetown-Fall River State Forest
7. Garden in the Woods
8. Acton Arboretum
9. Nashua River Rail Trail
10. Wachusett Mountain State Reservation
11. The Botanic Garden of Smith College
12. Mount Holyoke Range State Park
13. Mount Sugarloaf State Reservation
14. Savoy Mountain State Forest
15. Jacob's Ladder Trail
16. Bish Bash Falls State Park
17. Berkshire Botanical Garden
18. Pittsfield State Forest
19. Appalachian National Scenic Trail
20. Mohawk Trail State Forest
21. Arnold Arboretum
22. Elm Bank Horticulture Center

Measurements denote the height of plants unless otherwise indicated. Illustrations are not to scale.

N.B. – Many edible wild plants have poisonous mimics. Never eat a wild plant or fruit unless you are absolutely sure it is safe to do so. The publisher makes no representation or warranties with respect to the accuracy, completeness, correctness or usefulness of this information and specifically disclaims any implied warranties of fitness for a particular purpose. The advice, strategies and/or techniques contained herein may not be suitable for all individuals. The publisher shall not be responsible for any physical harm (up to and including death), loss of profit or other commercial damage. The publisher assumes no liability brought or instituted by individuals or organizations arising out of or relating in any way to the application and/or use of the information, advice and strategies contained herein.

Made in the USA

Waterford Press publishes reference guides that introduce readers to nature observation, outdoor recreation and survival skills. Product information is featured on the website: **www.waterfordpress.com**

Text & illustrations © 2008, 2022 Waterford Press Inc. All rights reserved. Photos © Shutterstock. Ecoregion map © The National Atlas of the United States. To order or for information on custom published products please call 800-434-2555 or email orderdesk@waterfordpress.com. For permissions or to share comments email editor@waterfordpress.com.

ISBN 978-1-58355-412-8 $7.95 U.S.
50795
9 781583 554128
UPC
8 84682 01025 6
10 9 8 7 6 5 4 3 2 1 2210511

MASSACHUSETTS TREES & WILDFLOWERS

A POCKET NATURALIST® GUIDE

MASSACHUSETTS TREES & WILDFLOWERS

A Folding Pocket Guide to Familiar Plants

Waterford Press

T0124003

Red Pine
Pinus resinosa To 80 ft. (24 m)
Flexible needles are up to 6 in. (15 cm) long and grow in bundles of two. Common in sandy soils.

Red Spruce
Picea rubens To 80 ft. (24 m)
Note conical crown of silhouette. 4-sided flattened needles have sharp points and grow singly along branchlets.

Eastern White Pine
Pinus strobus To 100 ft. (30 m)
Needles grow in bundles of 5. Cone is up to 8 in. (20 cm) long.

Pitch Pine
Pinus rigida To 60 ft. (18 m)
Long needles grow in bundles of 3. Cone scales have stiff, curved spines. Bark is rich with resin (pitch).

Eastern Redcedar
Juniperus virginiana To 60 ft. (18 m)
4-sided branchlets are covered with overlapping, scale-like leaves. Fruit is a blue berry.

Eastern Hemlock
Tsuga canadensis To 70 ft. (21 m)
Flat needles grow from 2 sides of twigs, parallel to the ground. Tip of tree usually droops.

Tamarack
Larix laricina To 80 ft. (24 m)
Needles grow in tufts. Stalkless cones grow upright. One of the only conifers to shed its needles in winter.

Atlantic White-cedar
Chamaecyparis thyoides
To 90 ft. (27 m)
Slender twigs have opposite, scale-like leaves. Tiny cones grow to .25 in. (.6 cm) long.

Striped Maple
Acer pensylvanicum To 30 ft. (9 m)
Shrub or small tree is distinguished by its white-striped, bright green bark.

Red Maple
Acer rubrum To 90 ft. (27 m)
Leaves have 3-5 lobes and turn scarlet in autumn. Flowers are succeeded by red, winged seed pairs.

Sugar Maple
Acer saccharum To 100 ft. (30 m)
Leaves have five coarsely-toothed lobes. Fruit is a winged seed pair. Tree sap is the source of maple syrup.

Silver Maple
Acer saccharinum To 80 ft. (24 m)
Note short trunk and spreading crown. 5-lobed leaves are silvery beneath.

Trembling Aspen
Populus tremuloides To 70 ft. (21 m)
Long-stemmed leaves rustle in the slightest breeze. The most widely distributed tree in North America.

Eastern Cottonwood
Populus deltoides To 100 ft. (30 m)
Leaves are up to 7 in. (18 cm) long. Flowers are succeeded by capsules containing seeds with cottony 'tails.'

Boxelder
Acer negundo To 60 ft. (18 m)
Leaves have 3-7 leaflets. Seeds are encased in paired papery keys.

Green Ash
Fraxinus pennsylvanica
To 60 ft. (18 m)
Leaves have 7-9 leaflets. Flowers are succeeded by clusters of single-winged fruits.

Black Birch
Betula lenta To 80 ft. (24 m)
Leaves are saw-toothed. Twigs smell like wintergreen. Dark bark is brown to blackish.

Paper Birch
Betula papyrifera To 70 ft. (21 m)
Whitish bark peels off trunk in thin sheets. Bark was used by Native Americans to make bowls and canoes.

American Beech
Fagus grandifolia To 80 ft. (24 m)
Flowers bloom in rounded clusters in spring and are succeeded by 3-sided nuts.

Alder
Alnus spp. To 40 ft. (12 m)
Shrub or tree often forms dense thickets. Flowers bloom in long clusters and are succeeded by distinctive, cone-like woody fruits.

Flowering Dogwood
Cornus florida To 30 ft. (9 m)
Tiny yellow flowers bloom in crowded clusters surrounded by 4 white petal-like structures.

Eastern Hophornbeam
Ostrya virginiana To 50 ft. (15 m)
Trunk has sinewy, muscle-like bark. Hop-like fruits are hanging, cone-like clusters.

American Hornbeam
Carpinus caroliniana To 30 ft. (9 m)
Also called blue beech, it has blue-gray bark and a 'muscular' trunk. Distinctive fruits have seeds contained in 3-sided bracts.

Butternut
Juglans cinerea To 70 ft. (21 m)
Leaves have 11-17 leaflets. Oval fruits are 4-ribbed.

American Plum
Prunus americana To 30 ft. (9 m)
Oval leaves have toothed edges. Bright red fruits have yellow flesh.

Black Tupelo
Nyssa sylvatica To 100 ft. (30 m)
Glossy leaves turn red in autumn. Blue fruits have ridged seeds.

Shagbark Hickory
Carya ovata To 100 ft. (30 m)
Bark curls away from the trunk, giving it a shaggy appearance. Leaves have 5 leaflets.

Bitternut Hickory
Carya cordiformis To 80 ft. (24 m)
Leaves have 7-11 leaflets. Twigs end in yellow buds. Bitter fruits are unpalatable to most wildlife.

Black Cherry
Prunus serotina To 80 ft. (24 m)
Aromatic bark and leaves smell cherry-like. Dark berries have an oval stone inside. Found in SE.

White Oak
Quercus alba To 100 ft. (30 m)
Leaves have 5-9 rounded lobes. Acorn has a shallow, scaly cup.

Northern Red Oak
Quercus rubra To 90 ft. (27 m)
Large tree has a rounded crown. Leaves have 7-11 spiny lobes.

Black Oak
Quercus velutina To 80 ft. (24 m)
Leaves have 5-7 spiny lobes. Acorns have a ragged-edged cup.

Black Willow
Salix nigra To 100 ft. (30 m)
Tree or shrub, often leaning. Slender leaves are shiny green on the upper surface. Flowers bloom in long, fuzzy clusters.

American Mountain-ash
Sorbus americana To 30 ft. (9 m)
Leaves have 13-17 leaflets. Red fruits occur in dense clusters.

American Basswood
Tilia americana To 100 ft. (30 m)
Leaves are heart-shaped. Flowers and nutlets hang from narrow leafy bracts.

American Elm
Ulmus americana To 100 ft. (30 m)
Note vase-shaped profile. Leaves are toothed. Fruits have a papery collar and are notched at the tip.
Massachusetts' state tree.

Common Juniper
Juniperus communis To 4 ft. (1.2 m)
Needle-like leaves grow in whorls of 3 around twigs. Berry-like, blue-black cones have 1-3 seeds.

Witch Hazel
Hamamelis virginiana To 30 ft. (9 m)
Shrub or small tree. Leaves turn yellow in autumn. Fruits are woody capsules with 4 sharp points.

Pussy Willow
Salix discolor To 20 ft. (6 m)
Distinctive fuzzy catkins appear in spring before the leaves.

Rhododendron
Rhododendron maximum To 40 ft. (12 m)
Evergreen leaves are thick and leathery. White to pink flowers bloom in dense clusters.

Spicebush
Lindera benzoin
To 17 ft. (5.1 m)
Shrub has small yellow flowers succeeded by bright red berries.

Smooth Sumac
Rhus glabra
To 20 ft. (6 m)
Clusters of white flowers are succeeded by 'hairy' red fruits. Bark is gray and smooth.

Mountain Laurel
Kalmia latifolia
To 20 ft. (6 m)
Evergreen shrub or small tree.
Leaves are leathery.

Buttonbush
Cephalanthus occidentalis
To 10 ft. (3 m)
'Pincushion' flowers have protruding stamens.

Northern Bush Honeysuckle
Diervilla lonicera
To 4 ft. (1.2 m)

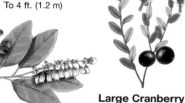

Highbush Blueberry
Vaccinium corymbosum
To 15 ft. (4.5 m)
Grows in acidic soils.

Large Cranberry
Vaccinium macrocarpon
To 12 in. (30 cm)
Creeping shrub is found in boggy areas and is also grown commercially.

American Elder
Sambucus canadensis
To 16 ft. (4.8 cm)
Shrub or small tree. Saw-toothed leaves have 3-7 leaflets. Flowers are succeeded by dark berries.

WHITE & GREENISH FLOWERS

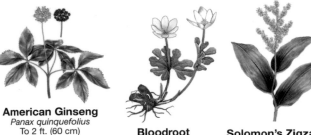

Gold Thread
Coptis trifolia
To 6 in. (15 cm)
Shiny basal leaves have 3 lobes. Brilliant, 5-petalled white flowers bloom in summer.

Wood Anemone
Anemone quinquefolia
To 8 in. (20 cm)
Found in moist meadows and woods.

Pearly Everlasting
Anaphalis margaritacea
To 3 ft. (90 cm)
Creamy flowers bloom in large terminal clusters.

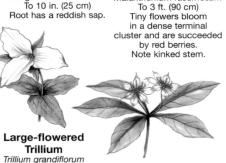

Foam Flower
Tiarella cordifolia
To 12 in. (30 cm)

Dutchman's Breeches
Dicentra cucullaria
To 12 in. (30 cm)
Spurred flowers resemble trousers.

Daisy Fleabane
Erigeron annuus
To 5 ft. (1.5 m)
Flowers are white to pinkish or purple.

Wild Leek
Allium tricoccum
To 20 in. (50 cm)
Harvest pungent bulbs and prepare like onions.

Mayflower
Epigaea repens
Stems to 16 in. (40 cm)
Creeping plant has pink or white flowers.
Massachusetts' state wildflower.

Bunchberry
Cornus canadensis
To 8 in. (20 cm)
Leaves grow in whorls of 4-6. Small white flowers are succeeded by bright red berries.

Boneset
Eupatorium perfoliatum
To 4 ft. (1.2 m)
Hairy plant with stout, erect stem. Fuzzy, white flowers bloom in dense clusters.

Oxeye Daisy
Leucanthemum vulgare
To 3 ft. (90 cm)
Showy flowers bloom along roadsides in summer.

Wild Strawberry
Fragaria spp.
Stems to 8 in. (20 cm)
Creeping plant has 5-petalled flowers that are succeeded by the familiar fruit.

False Lily-of-the-valley
Maianthemum canadense
To 6 in. (15 cm)
Flowers bloom in a spire-like cluster.

WHITE & GREENISH FLOWERS

American Ginseng
Panax quinquefolius
To 2 ft. (60 cm)

Bloodroot
Sanguinaria canadensis
To 10 in. (25 cm)
Root has a reddish sap.

Solomon's Zigzag
Maianthemum racemosum
To 3 ft. (90 cm)
Tiny flowers bloom in a dense terminal cluster and are succeeded by red berries. Note kinked stem.

Queen Anne's Lace
Daucus carota
To 4 ft. (1.2 m)
Flower clusters become cup-shaped as they age.

Large-flowered Trillium
Trillium grandiflorum
To 18 in. (45 cm)
3 white petals turn pinkish with age.

Starflower
Trientalis borealis
To 8 in. (20 cm)

YELLOW & ORANGE FLOWERS

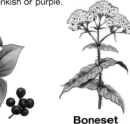

Butterfly Weed
Asclepias tuberosa
To 3 ft. (90 cm)
Orange flowers are star-shaped.

Orange Hawkweed
Hieracium aurantiacum
To 2 ft. (60 cm)
Hairy plant has leaves clustered at its base.

Bluebead Lily
Clintonia borealis
To 15 in. (38 cm)

Wild Indigo
Baptisia tinctoria
To 3 ft. (90 cm)

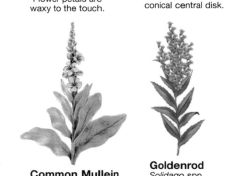
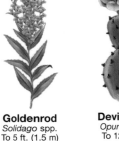

Seaside Goldenrod
Solidago sempervirens
To 8 ft. (2.4 m)
Grows in sandy soil and salt marshes.

Marsh Marigold
Caltha palustris
To 2 ft. (60 cm)

Dogtooth Violet
Erythronium americanum
To 10 in. (25 cm)
Common in meadows and rich woodlands.

YELLOW & ORANGE FLOWERS

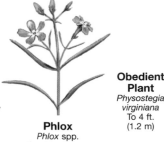

Day Lily
Hemerocallis fulva
To 4 ft. (1.2 m)

Yellow Flag
Iris pseudacorus
To 3 ft. (90 cm)

Wood Lily
Lilium philadelphicum
To 28 in. (70 cm)

Butter-and-Eggs
Linaria vulgaris
To 3 ft. (90 cm)
Spurred flowers have a patch of orange in the throat.

Shrubby Cinquefoil
Potentilla simplex
Stems to 3 ft. (90 cm)
Sprawling roadside plant has leaves with 5 leaflets.

Common Evening Primrose
Oenothera biennis
To 5 ft. (1.5 m)
Lemon-scented, 4-petalled flowers bloom in the evening.

Yellow Pond Lily
Nuphar spp.
Flower to 2.5 in. (6 cm) wide.
Floating aquatic plant.

Buttercup
Ranunculus spp.
To 3 ft. (90 cm)
Flower petals are waxy to the touch.

Black-eyed Susan
Rudbeckia hirta
To 3 ft. (90 cm)
Flower has a dark, conical central disk.

Downy Yellow Violet
Viola pubescens
To 16 in. (40 cm)

Common Mullein
Verbascum thapsus
To 7 ft. (2.1 m)
Common roadside weed.

Goldenrod
Solidago spp.
To 5 ft. (1.5 m)
Flowers bloom in arched clusters.

Devil's Tongue
Opuntia humifusa
To 12 in. (30 cm)
Clumps to 3 ft. (90 cm) wide.

PINK & RED FLOWERS

Columbine
Aquilegia canadensis
To 2 ft. (60 cm)

Wild Ginger
Asarum canadense
To 12 in. (30 cm)
Flowers arise at base of 2 leaves.

Common Milkweed
Asclepias syriaca
To 3 ft. (90 cm)
Pink-purple flowers bloom in drooping clusters.

Fireweed
Chamerion angustifolium
To 10 ft. (3 m)
Common in open woodlands and waste areas.

Bleeding Heart
Dicentra spp.
To 18 in. (45 cm)

Spring Beauty
Claytonia spp.
To 10 in. (25 cm)

Wild Geranium
Geranium maculatum
To 2 ft. (60 cm)

Joe-Pye Weed
Eutrochium maculatum
To 7 ft. (2.1 m)
Flowers are pink to purple. Leaves grow in whorls of 3-5.

Bull Thistle
Cirsium vulgare
To 6 ft. (1.8 m)

Pink Lady's Slipper
Cypripedium acaule
To 14 in. (35 cm)

Dame's Rocket
Hesperis matronalis
To 4 ft. (1.2 m)

Cardinal Flower
Lobelia cardinalis
To 4 ft. (1.2 m)

Rose Pogonia
Pogonia ophioglossoides
To 2 ft. (60 cm)

PINK & RED FLOWERS

Trumpet Honeysuckle
Lonicera sempervirens
Vine to 17 ft. (5.1 m)

Phlox
Phlox spp.
To 20 in. (50 cm)
Five-petalled, yellow-centered flowers may be white, yellow, pink, red or lavender. Grows in sprawling clusters.

Obedient Plant
Physostegia virginiana
To 4 ft. (1.2 m)

Red Clover
Trifolium pratense
To 2 ft. (60 cm)
Leaves have 3 leaflets.

Painted Trillium
Trillium undulatum
To 20 in. (50 cm)

Virginia Meadow Beauty
Rhexia virginica
To 2 ft. (60 cm)
Pink flowers have 8 yellow stamens.

BLUE & PURPLE FLOWERS

Jack-in-the-Pulpit
Arisaema triphyllum
To 3 ft. (90 cm)
Club-like stem is surrounded by a curving, green to purplish hood.

Common Morning Glory
Ipomoea purpurea
Stems to 10 ft. (3 m) long.
Creeping plant.

Bluets
Houstonia caerulea
To 6 in. (15 cm)
Yellow-centered flowers grow in large colonies.

New England Aster
Symphyotrichum novae-angliae
To 7 ft. (2.1 m)

Asiatic Dayflower
Commelina communis
To 3 ft. (90 cm)
Flowers have two large blue petals above a tiny white one.

Blue Flag
Iris versicolor
To 3 ft. (90 cm)

BLUE & PURPLE FLOWERS

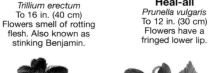

Blue Vervain
Verbena hastata
To 6 ft. (1.8 m)
Has a slender spike of bluish flowers.

Purple Loosestrife
Lythrum salicaria
To 7 ft. (2.1 m)
Invasive weed is very common in marshes and ponds.

Virginia Spiderwort
Tradescantia virginiana
To 3 ft. (90 cm)

Periwinkle
Vinca minor
To 8 in. (20 cm)
Mat-forming plant.

Creeping Bellflower
Campanula rapunculoides
To 3 ft. (90 cm)

Red Trillium
Trillium erectum
To 16 in. (40 cm)
Flowers smell of rotting flesh. Also known as stinking Benjamin.

Heal-all
Prunella vulgaris
To 12 in. (30 cm)
Flowers have a fringed lower lip.

True Forget-me-not
Myosotis scorpioides
To 2 ft. (60 cm)
Small sky-blue flowers have yellow centers.

Fringed Gentian
Gentianopsis crinita
To 3 ft. (90 cm)

Common Blue Violet
Viola sororia
To 8 in. (20 cm)

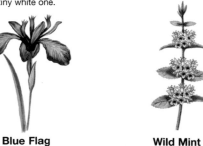

Wild Mint
Mentha arvensis
To 31 in. (78 cm)

Blueweed
Echium vulgare
To 30 in. (75 cm)
Blue flowers have long, red stamens. Also called viper's bugloss.

Wild Blue Lupine
Lupinus perennis
To 2 ft. (60 cm)
Note star-shaped leaves.